I0605916

The Exemplary Life of Emir Abd al-Qadir al-Jazairy

Illustrated by **Demi**

with

Afeefa Syeed and Tamar Miller

The Exemplary Life of Emir Abd al-Qadir al-Jazairy

Afeefa Syeed Demi Tamar Miller

First published in 2025 by
Fons Vitae
49 Mockingbird Valley Drive
Louisville, KY 40207
http://www.fonsvitae.com
Email: fonsvitaeky@aol.com

Library of Congress Control Number: 2025940739

ISBN 979-8-89640-005-9

Printed in Canada

YouTube videos about Abd al-Qadir
Filip Holm, "Let's Talk Religion", 60 minutes
https://www.youtube.com

Podcast about Emir Abd al-Qadir:
Dr Lahouari Ramzi Taleb, The Hikmah Project, 2 hours and 15 minutes
https://www.thehikmahproject.com

Foreword

This is a true story—told in the imagined voice of one of the 19th century's most extraordinary figures, Emir Abd al-Qadir al-Jazairy. Crafted especially for children, their parents, and educators, we invite readers of all ages to discover the exemplary life of the Emir, an Islamic scholar, humanitarian, warrior, and poet—a man who embodied harmony between inner conviction and outward action, even in the face of great adversity, and who combined spirituality with justice.

A celebration of character, courage, and compassion, the story is brought to life through evocative illustrations that reflect both the nobility of Emir Abd al-Qadir and the rich world that shaped him—and which he, in turn, helped to shape.

Fons Vitae is honored to present the work of world-renowned children's illustrator DEMI, whose deep reverence for the artistic traditions of Islamic cultures shines throughout this volume. Her luminous illustrations, inspired by the art, clothing, and architecture of Islamic cultures worldwide, are rooted in rich visual legacies shaped by the life and example of the Prophet Muhammad ﷺ.

While not intended as literal historical recreations of 19th-century North Africa, where our story begins, these illustrations capture the essence and spirit of the broader Muslim world to which the Emir belonged—imbuing each page with beauty, imagination, and reverence.

The historical foundation of this biography, set in the Regency of Algiers, France, and Damascus, is drawn from *Commander of the Faithful: The Life and Times of Emir Abdelkader* by John W. Kiser.

بسم الله الرحمن الرحيم

Come… come… sit close.

I am Abd al-Qadir al-Jaza'iry. Today, I want to share with you stories from my life that helped me practice being kind, courageous, and good.

Let us keep our Hearts open and let the Light within each of us flow out to help others.

I was born in 1808 in a fertile valley called al-Hamam, nestled in the land of Algiers on the northern coast of Africa.

My family belongs to a Bedouin tribe descended from the Prophet Muhammad ﷺ. Though we did not have many things, we were rich in wisdom, contentment and inner strength.

Our parents expected my sisters, brothers, and me to be kind and to extend an open hand to everyone who came for help.

"Whatsoever direction you turn, there is the Presence of Allah."

Qur'an, 2:115

When we were very young, our mother, Zahra, taught my sister Khadija and me how to read, write, and sew neat stitches. We were excited to make our own clothes and loved reading many books together!

My father, Muhyi al-Din, was a leader and a teacher. He inherited a *zawiya*—a special place for study and spiritual gatherings.

There, as a young boy, I loved practicing writing in beautiful Arabic script.

My father invited me to meetings with wise elders, where I observed them solving problems for our community, such as figuring out how to care for people who fell sick.

I was grateful to live near the Sahara, a land full of secret wonders. We took great care of our horses, and when we rode, it felt like we were flying with the wind!

As I grew older, my friends and I joined our tribe's hunting expeditions. We helped provide food for our families, improved our horsemanship, and learned to respect the desert.

My father said: "A great leader, like a skilled hunter, must be patient, observant, and swift."

I loved nature and everything about our world. Living in the desert, we wanted to become as:

Clever as a fox
Agile as a falcon
Gentle as a sheep
Swift as a gazelle
Wise as an owl, and
Resilient as a date
palm tree.

By the time I was 14, I had memorized all the verses in the Holy Qur'an, and loved reciting them!

Because of this, my people gave me the respectful title of Hafiz, which means Protector. When I grew older, I earned an *ijaza*, a certificate that permitted me to interpret the Qur'an and teachings of Prophet Muhammad ﷺ.

Eager to learn more, I studied the ideas of important thinkers like Plato, Aristotle, Maimonides, and great Muslim scholars such as Averroes, Ibn Khaldun, Avicenna, al-Ghazali, and Ibn Taymiyya.

That was not all! Mathematics, the geography of the world, astronomy, and philosophy fascinated me. I even studied medicine for people as well as for animals.

My teachers often told me that I was good at public speaking and debates.

And to this day, I have always loved reading and writing poetry.

My beloved wife, Lalla Kheira, was an inspiration. Everyone cherished her kindness and sincerity. Marrying her was one of my greatest joys.

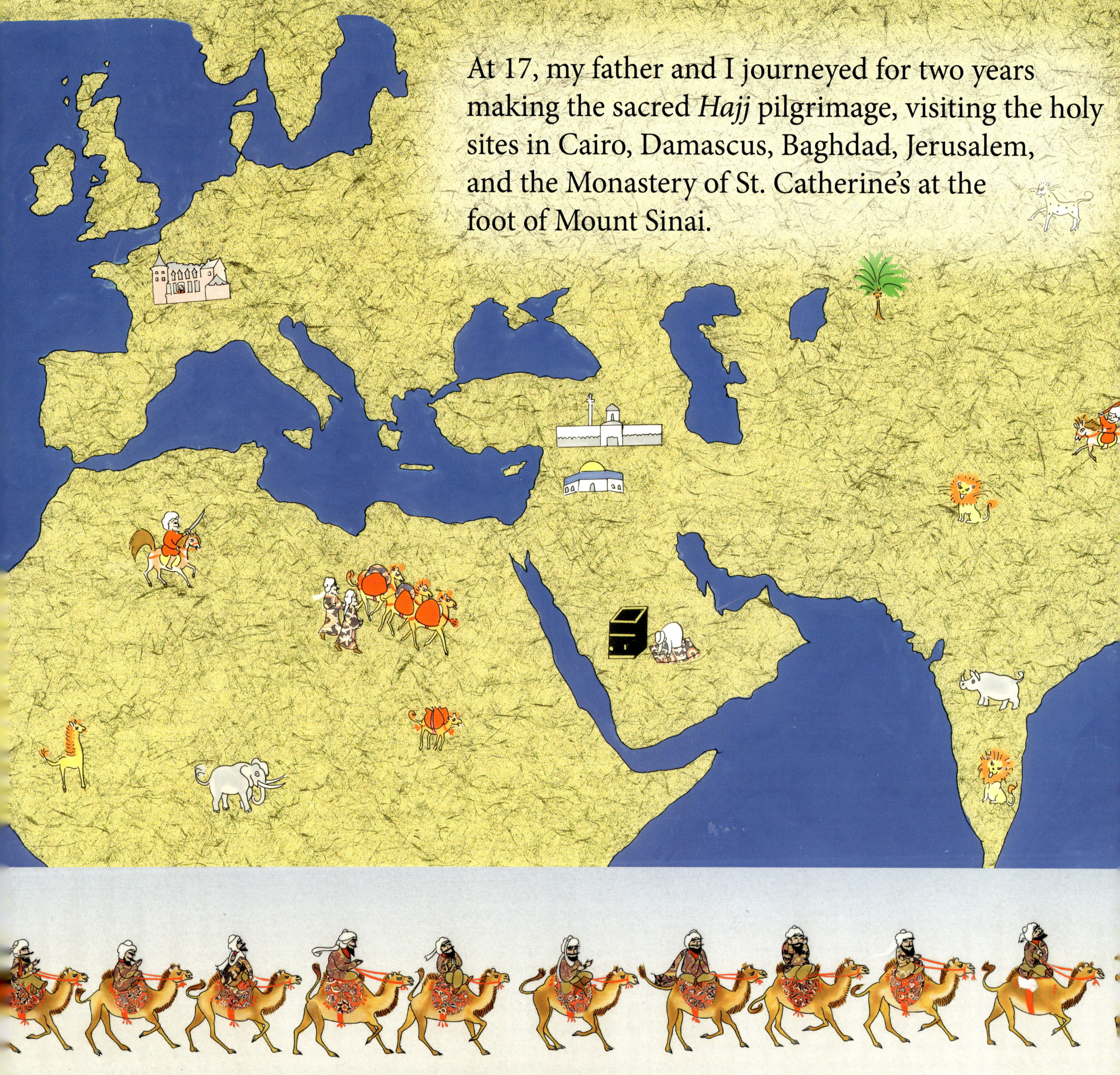

At 17, my father and I journeyed for two years making the sacred *Hajj* pilgrimage, visiting the holy sites in Cairo, Damascus, Baghdad, Jerusalem, and the Monastery of St. Catherine's at the foot of Mount Sinai.

In magnificent Cairo, I was deeply pleased to see how the leader Pasha Muhammad Ali improved the lives of people in his country by printing books and newspapers so that more people could learn to read.

As we arrived in Makkah, it felt like we were at the heart of the world. We greeted men and women from every land—Arabs, sub-Saharan Africans, Turks, Persians, Indians, Javanese, and even Tatars and Bukharans from Central Asia—all coming together in peace.

bateau سفينة
guerre حرب
maison بيت

When my father and I returned home in 1830, a lot had changed. The colonial army of France invaded and made unfair laws that hurt my people.

Some fled their homes and villages; others were forced to speak French rather than Arabic; and some were forced to change their last names. The invading army destroyed many mosques, too.

My father gathered the local tribes to decide what to do. They chose me to lead instead of my older brother, and I accepted with humility.

Some of our people wanted to fight, while others hoped to trade with the French. I sought a path that could unite us.

My first *jihad,* or struggle, was organizing a force to defend our rights and our freedom.

The second—and greater *jihad*—was to hold fast to our innate goodness, like a light in the darkness, and to endure hardship with patience and mercy.

With the job of Commander-in-Chief, I came to be known as Emir Abd al-Qadir.

The French Army in North Africa had 100,000 powerfully equipped men, outnumbering my army, which only had 10,000,

In battle, we cared for the land, animals, and even our enemies, just as the Prophet Muhammad ﷺ taught by his example.

One day, I saw that we didn't have enough food for the French soldiers that we had captured. This made me sad and I ordered their release so that they would not starve.

During this long war, Mascara became our protected city and we welcomed people from many lands. We were kind and respectful to each other.

We also created ways for everyone to have water, food, and shelter.

At a time when it was almost unheard of, we built a medical school for women who wanted to become doctors!

Every day, even during the fighting, I used my special rug, my *sajada*, for meditation and prayer.

Still today, these daily practices help me feel close to God.

I heard that the French officer and diplomat Léon Roches, said this:

> *'…Sometimes I had the honor of sleeping in Abd al-Qadir's tent and when I saw him deep in prayer in the middle of the night, he was the brightest image of faith and mystical devotion. I imagine the great Christian saints must have prayed this way.'*

Later, Roches—who spoke Arabic and began to understand our ways—helped me negotiate a truce, even though some of my countrymen wanted to keep fighting.

It was a hard decision, but by 1847, after fifteen years of struggle and much suffering for my people, I agreed to a truce.

The French colonial army would not leave our land, and continuing the fight would only bring more pain.

I chose what I believed was best for those I had vowed to protect.

Some thought I was giving up, but I felt it was wiser to end the war.

To show that I would keep my word and honor our agreement, I gave my sword and my beloved black horse to the French military leaders in my country.

My family, loyalists, and I agreed to leave Algiers, but only on one important condition: that we would be granted a safe journey to a land where mostly Muslims lived.

But King Louis-Philippe of France did not keep his promise. The French authorities argued about what to do with us, and by the time they made a decision, he was no longer king.

I appealed to the new ruler, Napoléon III, asking him to honor the promise made to me. But he, too, refused at first. Ninety-seven of my family members and closest companions had to leave Algeria, our beloved home, and together we were taken away by boat.

We were moved from place to place in France and ended up in the Chateau d'Amboise under 'house arrest,' unable to leave.

It was so cold and damp that members of my family got very sick. Twenty-five of them even died. You can imagine the pain and sadness that I felt inside.

French General Eugene Daumas said:

"The Emir never complains for himself, though he is determined to hold France to its word. He forgives his enemies, even those who can still make him suffer, and he will not allow anyone to speak ill of them in his presence."

Sister Natalie, a French nun, wrote a letter to her Christian community telling them that she would be happy to spend the rest of her life serving us because we stayed calm and dignified, even in terribly harsh conditions.

After five years, the French Emperor Louis Napoleon III finally freed us, but we were never to be allowed to return home to Algeria.

"You have been an enemy of France", he said to me, "but I respect your courage and your character … this is why I must bring your captivity to an end, trusting you entirely because you have given your word."

The French leader invited me and some of my family and loyalists to the theater, the palace, and the famous Cathedral of Notre Dame. Everywhere we went, people wanted to meet and embrace us.

Before leaving France, the Emperor presented me with 150,000 francs and a white horse, as compensation—a kind of apology, though this could never make up for the terrible things that had happened to us.

Finally, we arrived in Damascus, where we were warmly welcomed. What a profound relief that I could now devote myself to writing, teaching, and a life of contemplation.

It was inspiring to live next to the burial place of the saintly Ibn al-Arabi, who lived 700 hundred years before me. He said:

"My religion is that of love, and wherever my caravans head, Love is my religion and my faith."

I was deeply pleased to be with young people, elders, and my family, as I taught from sacred texts and the writings of great spiritual teachers. Just as I had done in my father's *zawiya*, we had spiritual conversations where everyone listened with care and paid attention with deep respect. What pleased me most was that we spoke from the Heart.

But then, in 1860, I began to hear troubling rumors—whispers that violence was brewing. I tried to warn the rulers in Damascus. When the unrest finally broke out, we opened our home as a place of refuge for French diplomats, Jewish families, and Christians—amont them the Sisters of Mercy.

My family and followers helped save the lives of nearly 10,000 people!

When a French Bishop of Algiers wrote me a thank you letter, I explained:

> *"What I did for the Christians, I did because of my faith as a Muslim. All religions brought to us by the prophets, from Adam until Muhammad ﷺ rest on two principles—praise for God and compassion for all His creatures."*

At 55, I returned to Makkah. I prayed deeply and for a long time beside the Kaaba, the most sacred sanctuary in Islam.

When everyone else was asleep, I became aware of a Protective Nearness surrounding me. I was filled with gratitude for all the blessings I have been given in my life.

I meditated in Hira, the very cave where the angel Gabriel delivered the Qur'an to the Prophet Muhammad ﷺ.

I was reminded of the Prophetic saying: "The ink of the scholar is worth more than the blood of martyrs." At that moment, I vowed to live a life of learning, anchored in kindness and guided by mercy.

إِنَّا لِلَّٰهِ وَإِنَّا إِلَيْهِ رَاجِعُونَ

In 1883, Emir Abd al-Qadir died. When Muslims hear of someone's death, they say: "*Surely we belong to God and surely unto God is our Return.*"

Everyone who met the Emir recognized his extraordinary Presence.

He taught that each of us carries a Light within, which is our natural goodness or *fitrah*—our inner pure state of being. We, too, can be kind and wise when we become aware of this Light, nurture it, and live by it.

May the exemplary life of Abd al-Qādir help us use this Light to create peace in our hearts and offer peace to others.

A Gallery of images from Emir Abd al-Qadir's Life

"Emir Abd al-Qadir gave, early and without prior knowledge, a faithful description of what now constitutes the daily work of the delegates of the International Committee of International Humanitarian Law: to support prisoners and ensure respect for their rights, as well as to reassure their families."

– Former President of the International Committee of the Red Cross, Jakob Kellberger

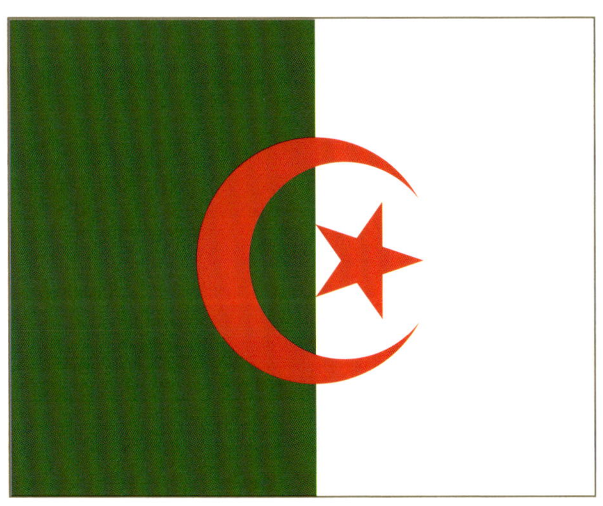

Emir Abd al-Qadir is considered the father of modern Algeria. In 1963, his body was returned to Algeria, a year after independence.

A Bridge ov the Turkey River, in the American town of Elkader, Iowa, which was thus named in honor of the Emir Abd al-Qadir.

Legacies

Abd al-Qadir's literary works span from the book *Horses of the Sahara* to Islamic jurisprudence as well as commentary on Ibn Arabi who was an inspiration for him throughout his life.

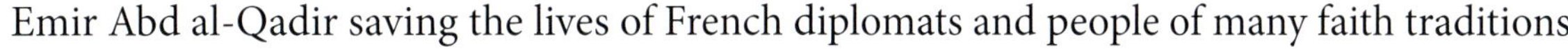

Emir Abd al-Qadir saving the lives of French diplomats and people of many faith traditions.

Honors

Emir Abd al-Qadir is recognized as a great peacemaker. He was bestowed:

The Grand Cross of the Legion of Honor from France.

A Star of Magnificence from the Masonic Order, universalists at the time.

The Grand Cross of the Redeemer from the Greeks.

The Order of the Medjidie from the Turks.

The Order of Pope Pius IX from the Vatican.

Two Colt pistols were sent by the American President.

Honored in Paris by Emperor Napoleon III.

H.M. Queen Victoria of Great Britain.

The New York Times eulogized him as "one of the great men of the century."

This is the seal of the Emirate of Mascara, which was a sovereign state founded by Emir Abd al-Qadir al-Jazairy with the allegiance of the people of Algeria to resist the French conquest of the country, with its first capital at Mascara, then Tagdemt after it was taken by France.

With gratitude to John W. Kiser
author of
Commander of the Faithful:
The Life and Times of Emir Abdelkader
A Story of True Jihad

May this beautifully presented story, crafted for the youth of our world, also inspire adults to think and act in the spirit of Abdelkader.